Skits from Scripture
10 Plays from the
New Testament

Page McKean Zyromski

Pflaum Publishing Group
Dayton, OH 45439

Skits from Scripture
10 Plays from the
New Testament

Page McKean Zyromski

Cover and Interior Design by Ellen Wright
Edited by Karen Cannizzo

Second Printing: 2008

Pflaum Publishing Group
2621 Dryden Road, Suite 300
Dayton, OH 45439
800-543-4383
www.pflaum.com

ISBN 978-0-937997-97-0

Contents

Introduction

I never taught a group that didn't enjoy reading plays. Sixth and seventh graders even write skits of their own when scripts aren't available. This brings up the problem of biblical accuracy (instead of enthusiasm alone) and the reason for this book.

Skits from Scripture: 10 Plays from the New Testament offers reproducible Bible-based skits that have been tested with young people. Helps for the dedicated director (usually this is you-know-who) are included.

If taken in sequence, these plays can give your group a quick overview of the sweep of New Testament events, from Gabriel's visit to Mary through the death of Paul in Rome about 67 AD.

The plays were designed to fit three typical situations. In the first kind of situation, young people with speaking parts remain seated within the group. Since these skits are reproducible, everyone will have a script and follow along. Stage directions don't need to be read aloud because everyone can read them silently.

At other times, young people with speaking parts stand in front of the group, scripts in hand. They wear paper headbands or signs around their necks to indicate their roles. Scenery and place names are drawn on the chalkboard or on sheets of newsprint. Actors approach or leave these scenes as indicated in the script. "Stage right" is to the actors' right as they face the audience, "upstage" is farther from the audience, "downstage" is closer. Actors need to be discouraged from simply standing woodenly in place. The narrator should be a good reader, someone who will not stumble over strange words.

Finally we have the group that wants to present the skit to another group of young people, a parent group, or the congregation. Or the group that will use these skits as part of vacation Bible school. They use props as suggested in the Notes for the Director, pages 30-32. For costumes they use bright pieces of fabric draped over one shoulder and tied at the waist (both sexes). Girls may wear veils. Signs are used for place names and scenery. Like the young people pictured on the cover of this book, young actors can be encouraged to contribute their ideas and create props and costumes. But it's good to remember that if the presentations are kept simple, they'll be more enjoyable and young people will want to do them more often.

The difference between reading a skit within a group and presenting it to others is the amount of time required for rehearsing and the need for memorizing stage directions and speeches.

I've found a few techniques that keep things running smoothly. *Before* handing out scripts, I go over pronunciation of characters' names. If I don't hold back the scripts while I do this, young people ignore me and start reading silently. I also go over unfamiliar vocabulary words, which are listed and defined as Key Words for each skit in the Notes for the Director.

I remind actors to stand up straight, to speak with expression and a little more slowly than they think necessary. If they're performing the skit for others, actors have to be reminded not to turn their backs to the audience and never to upstage another actor who's speaking. From skit to skit I keep a list of who played each role so that eventually everyone gets a good speaking part.

One last suggestion before the curtain is raised. There are many ways to enrich the learning experiences young people will have in acting out these skits. You may, for example, create a game using the Key Words in each skit, and use the game as reinforcement for the story. Choose six to ten of the Key Words from a skit and write these words, along with their definitions, on two sets of 6" x 9" index cards. Spread both sets out face down, and have the young people play "Concentration." Gather the group in a large circle around the cards. Each player gets a chance to turn over two cards, reading each out loud. If the cards are a pair, the player keeps the cards. If not, the player turns the cards face down again, in the same places. Explain that everyone needs to pay attention so that they can remember where cards are located. Everyone

takes turns until all the cards have been collected by players. The player with the most cards at the end of the game wins. Consider allowing the winner to pick his or her role in the next skit.

Another way to enrich the experience for young people is to have them locate the places mentioned in the skits. Before young people begin to prepare a skit, they can be encouraged to find these places on a map of biblical sites and on a current world map or globe.

Not only do such activities help young people learn unfamiliar pronunciation, words, and places, but the activities also enliven your meetings with young people and, more importantly, nurture their knowledge and love of the Bible.

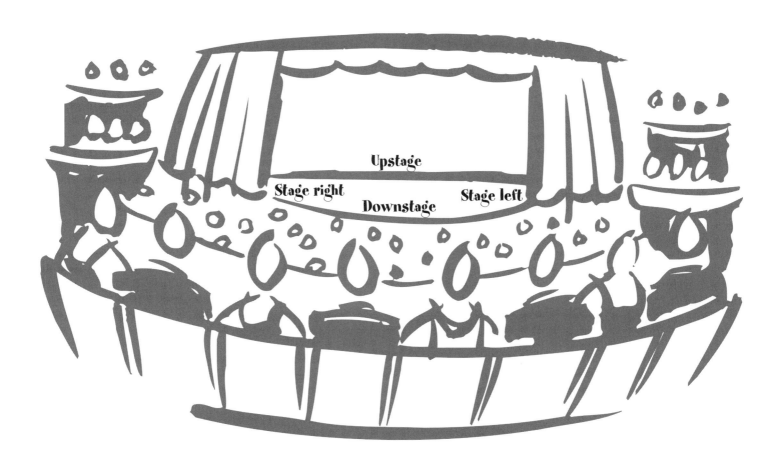

Mary–Journeying with Jesus

Narrator: The story of Jesus begins with a young girl about fourteen years old, Mary of Nazareth. From Christmas cards, we're all familiar with scenes of Bethlehem, the manger, and the shepherds. But the events that followed aren't as well known. Eight days after the shepherds came, Joseph and Mary presented Jesus in the temple, as all devout Jews used to do with their firstborn sons. *(Mary and Joseph enter from stage left. Mary holds the baby Jesus.)*

Joseph: *(as they cross to center stage)* Mary, I arranged for the sacrifice of two doves. It didn't cost as much as I thought it would.

Mary: I'm glad it went so quickly. Didn't you think it was noisy out there in the courtyard?

Joseph: It's a lot quieter in here. *(points to Simeon, who enters from stage right)* That old man over there looks like such a holy person. I wonder if he's a prophet.

Simeon: *(crosses to them and exclaims)* Ah, look at this child! He's the one I've been waiting for all my life! I know it! *(takes the baby from Mary and lifts his eyes to heaven)* Lord, you can let your servant go in peace now! My eyes have seen what you promised me!

Joseph: *(to Mary)* How great God is! He told this old man about Jesus!

Simeon: *(gives the baby to Mary and places his hands on Mary and Joseph's heads to bless them)* This child will bring the rise and fall of many. Some will speak against him. *(to Mary)* A sword will pierce your heart. *(Mary bows her head.)*

Anna: *(enters from stage right and hobbles over to Simeon)* Is this the child we've been waiting for? *(She lays her hand on Jesus.)* God be praised! *(turns to leave)* I must go tell the others who've been praying for this day! *(exits stage right, followed by Simeon; Mary and Joseph walk to stage left.)*

Joseph: *(holding Mary's arm)* Mary, what does all this mean? *(As they exit, Mary is shaking her head in wonder.)*

Narrator: While all this was happening, some astrologers in the east discovered a new star in the sky. They followed it until it stopped over Bethlehem, the place where Jesus, Mary, and Joseph were staying.

1st Wise Man: *(enters stage right)* We're getting closer. The star has stopped right over there. *(points stage left)*

2nd Wise Man: That's what it seems. Isn't it strange for such a great king to be born in an out-of-the-way place like this? *(makes a sweeping gesture around him)*

3rd Wise Man: Yes, it is, but we've seen many strange things in our lives. Who are we to question the ways of the All-powerful One?

1st Wise Man: I still wish we hadn't told Herod that we'd go back and tell him when we find this new king. I don't trust Herod.

2nd Wise Man: We can always go home a different way. The All-powerful One has guided us this far. He won't abandon us now.

3rd Wise Man: *(as they move stage left)* We're almost there. Do you think our gifts are good enough for the new king? *(They exit.)*

Narrator: The Wise Men were right to mistrust King Herod. An angel told them in a dream not to tell him about finding Jesus. Herod was angry. He ordered all baby boys under age two to be murdered.

Mary: *(enters from stage left, with the baby and Joseph)* Joseph, why do we have to leave so quickly? Couldn't we wait 'til morning?

Joseph: No, we can't wait! An angel told me in a dream that King Herod is sending soldiers to kill the child! We must go at once!

Mary: *(shocked)* To kill Jesus?

Joseph: You've heard about Herod. He's cruel!

Mary: Where will we go? Back to Nazareth?

Joseph: No, not yet. The angel said to flee to Egypt. Herod has no power there. We'll stay 'til Herod dies, then we'll go back to Nazareth. Don't worry, Mary. God will take care of us. *(They exit stage right.)*

Narrator: A few years later King Herod died, and Jesus, Mary, and Joseph were finally able to go back to Nazareth and live a quiet life.

Later, when Jesus was twelve years old, the holy family made a trip with others from Nazareth to Jerusalem for Passover. It was the custom for men and women to travel in different groups. *(A group of men, including Joseph, enters from stage right, followed by a group of women, including Mary. The groups meet center stage.)*

Mary: *(leaves the women and runs to Joseph)* Joseph! The festival this year was wonderful! Didn't you think so?

Joseph: Yes, but I'm tired. I'll be glad to get home.

Mary: *(looks around)* Where's Jesus? Did he enjoy it, too?

Joseph: Isn't he with you?

Mary: No, I thought he was with you and the men.

Joseph: But I thought he was with you! He's not with us.

Mary: If he's not with you and not with me, that means we left him in Jerusalem! He's lost!

Joseph: We'd better go back and find him! *(They exit stage right.)*

Narrator: For three days Mary and Joseph searched the city of Jerusalem. *(Jesus and a group of rabbis enter from stage left and stand, talking and gesturing. Mary and Joseph, looking very weary, enter from stage right.)*

Joseph: We've looked all over Jerusalem for him, Mary. I don't know what to do next.

Mary: I'm so worried! Where can he be?

Joseph: Let's go to the temple. Maybe somebody there has seen him. *(They cross the stage.)*

Mary: *(points to Jesus)* Joseph! Look! Listening to the rabbis! It's Jesus! But he's only twelve years old!

Joseph: These are the greatest teachers in Jerusalem! What does he think he's doing? Hurry! *(They approach Jesus.)*

Mary: Son, why have you done this to us? Your father and I've been so worried! We've been looking all over for you!

Jesus: Why did you have to go looking? Didn't you know I'd be in my Father's house? *(He crosses to stage right.)*

Joseph: *(to Mary)* Do you understand what he means by "my Father's house"?

Mary: No. I need time to think about all this. *(They exit stage right.)*

Narrator: Back home in Nazareth Jesus grew up and became a carpenter like Joseph. One day when Jesus was about thirty years old and Joseph had already died, Jesus and Mary were invited to a wedding in the town of Cana. At that time wedding celebrations lasted several days.

Philip: *(enters from stage right, with Nathaniel and other wedding guests, including Mary and Jesus)* Nathaniel, isn't this a fine wedding? Let's drink to the bride and groom! *(He lifts his goblet.)*

Nathaniel: *(clinks his goblet with Philip's)* I think more people are here than our host expected. The wine's getting low! *(They laugh, then walk center stage, where the Groom and Wine Steward are standing. Wedding guests stand and talk stage right.)*

Mary: *(listens to a Worried Servant, who whispers to her that the wine is gone)* Don't worry. I'll see what can be done. *(She goes to Jesus, who is standing with the other guests, and beckons to him.)* Son, they're out of wine.

Jesus: How does this involve me? My time hasn't come yet. *(He begins to turn away, but Mary touches his sleeve and looks at him intently.)*

Mary: *(calls to the 1st Servant and 2nd Servant, who are standing near six large water jars)* Are those jars for water? *(She points to Jesus.)* Do whatever he tells you.

Jesus: *(pauses, then speaks to the servants)* Fill the jars with water. Then dip some out and take it to the wine steward. *(He turns away and talks to the wedding guests. The servants dip a goblet into the water and take a sample to the Wine Steward, who is standing center stage, with the Groom.)*

Wine Steward: *(sips from the goblet)* Ah! Excellent, excellent! *(claps the Groom on the back)* Everybody else serves the best wine first, but you've saved the best till last! *(laughs)*

Groom: *(sips from the goblet)* It's very good, isn't it?

1st Servant: *(turns and walks stage right with the 2nd Servant)* Did you hear that? The water in those jars was changed to wine!

2nd Servant: Who's the man who told us to fill the jars?

1st Servant: He's from Nazareth. His name's Jesus. Let's go tell our friends about this!

2nd Servant: I've heard about this man before. *(They exit.)*

Narrator: That was the first of Jesus' miracles. There would be many more. Mary, Jesus' first and best disciple, continued to be present in her son's life all the way to the cross. Truly, every generation calls her blessed.

Elizabeth—Believing and Praising God

Narrator: Mary's cousin Elizabeth was married to a man named Zechariah. They lived in the hill country outside Jerusalem. Zechariah was a priest serving at the temple on a regular schedule. *(Elizabeth and her Maidservant enter from stage right.)*

Elizabeth: *(places her hand on her back)* Rain must be coming! The ache in my back is always a sign. I wonder where my husband is. His work in the temple is taking longer than usual this time.

Maidservant: *(points stage left)* I think he's coming now, Ma'am. And two other priests are with him.

Elizabeth: Do you think something's wrong? Why is he moving his hands like that? *(Zechariah enters from stage left, gesturing helplessly, pointing to his mouth. Two priests follow.)*

1st Priest: Elizabeth, I'm sorry to tell you that Zechariah hasn't been able to talk. We don't know why.

2nd Priest: Something happened when he took his turn in the temple. He's tried to tell us, but he can't.

1st Priest: He took so long in the sanctuary that we were worried. It's strange, but I think he might have had a vision or something.

2nd Priest: I hope his speech will come back. Send us a message if we can help. *(They exit stage left.)*

Elizabeth: *(to her Maidservant as Zechariah makes writing gestures)* Quick! Bring his wax tablet. It's over there in the corner. He wants to write something down. *(to Zechariah as the Maidservant brings the tablet)* What happened, Zechariah?

Elizabeth: *(pauses as Zechariah writes, then reads over his shoulder)* An angel appeared to you in the temple? Really! While you were serving? *(Zechariah erases and then writes more.)*

Elizabeth: *(pauses and reads)* The angel said that I'll have a son and we'll name him John? But Zechariah, I'm not able to have children. We're both too old now! *(Zechariah erases and writes more.)*

Elizabeth: *(pauses and reads)* The child will be filled with the Holy Spirit? Like the prophet Elijah? Oh, Zechariah, what's God doing for us! *(Zechariah writes more.)*

Elizabeth: *(pauses and reads)* And that's why you're not able to talk? Because you didn't believe what the angel said? He said your speech will come back when the child is born? Good! *(puts her arm around Zechariah)* Oh, Zechariah! I've waited so long to have a child! What a miracle that it's happening in our old age! *(They stand motionless as the Narrator reads.)*

Narrator: Shortly afterward Elizabeth conceived a child. All their relatives and friends were surprised, since none of them knew what the angel said in the temple. Six months later the angel Gabriel appeared to Mary at the annunciation, and Mary came immediately to see Elizabeth. *(Zechariah exits stage right. The Maidservant points stage left.)*

Maidservant: Your cousin Mary is at the gate, Ma'am. *(Elizabeth looks up, surprised.)*

Mary: *(enters from stage left)* Elizabeth! How are you? You look so well!

Elizabeth: *(puts her hands on her tummy)* Oh, Mary! Blessed are you among women and blessed is the child in your womb! As soon as I heard your voice, the baby in my womb jumped with joy!

Mary: *(hugs Elizabeth)* The Lord has done great things for me! Holy is his name!

Elizabeth: He's done wonderful things for me, too! *(pats her tummy again)*

Mary: I know! The angel Gabriel told me you were in your sixth month! I've come to help and to talk about how good the Lord is.

Elizabeth: Come in, come in! We have so much to talk about. Wait till I tell you what happened to Zechariah! You're the only person in the world who will really understand all this. Come in! You must be tired after such a long journey! *(She ushers Mary in. They stand motionless as the Narrator reads.)*

Narrator: Mary stayed with Elizabeth for three months. Together they marveled at all that God was doing. Finally the baby who would be known as John the Baptist was born. There was great excitement on the day of his circumcision. *(The Neighbor, Midwife, and Relative enter from stage right. The Midwife is holding the baby.)*

Neighbor: The day of a child's circumcision is a day of rejoicing.

Midwife: Yes, he's a healthy baby boy! God has been good to Elizabeth and Zechariah.

Neighbor: And now it's time for him to be given the sign of the covenant, the sign that marks us as children of Abraham!

Relative: And to name him Zechariah, after his father!

Elizabeth: *(puts her hand on Relative's sleeve)* No, his name is John!

Relative: That can't be. Nobody in our family has the name John. It's the custom to use names that are in the family!

Midwife: Ask Zechariah. He has the final word.

Neighbor: What good will that do? You know Zechariah hasn't been able to talk since his last time in the temple.

Relative: Here. He's been using this wax tablet to write things down. *(passes the tablet to Zechariah)* Zechariah, what are we to name the child? *(Zechariah writes and then holds up tablet.)*

Relative: *(reads)* "His name is John!" Well, what do you know!

Zechariah: *(begins to speak again, stammering at first)* It's J-J-John. Oh! I can speak again! My tongue is freed! Blessed be the God of Israel, he has come to the help of his people!

Elizabeth: Zechariah, you can talk! This is just what the angel said! Thanks be to God!

Zechariah: *(takes the baby from the Midwife and lifts the baby high)* You, my child, will be called a prophet of the Most High God. You will go ahead of the Lord to prepare the way for him.

Elizabeth: Everyone! We must all praise God for the wonderful things he is doing for all of us! *(The scene ends with all lifting arms in praise.)*

John the Baptist—Preparing the Way for Jesus

Narrator: Many months before Jesus began his public ministry, his cousin John the Baptist began preaching in the desert near the River Jordan. *(John enters from stage left, barefoot and dressed in rough clothing. The Soldier, Tax Collector, and Bystander enter from stage right, talking excitedly.)*

Soldier: What do you think of this new prophet? People from all over the country are coming to be baptized here in the River Jordan.

Tax Collector: I've heard he's the prophet Elijah who's supposed to return before the Messiah comes.

Soldier: He <u>looks</u> like Elijah in those clothes. They say he eats grasshoppers and wild honey.

Bystander: A friend told me he lives by strict rules. He never shaves or drinks any wine.

John: *(calls to them)* Come, turn away from your sins and be baptized! Change your lives. The kingdom of heaven is near!

Tax Collector: *(steps forward and kneels)* Teacher, what are we to do?

John: *(pretends to scoop water from the river to baptize the Tax Collector)* Receive this baptism with the resolution to change your life. Don't cheat any more. Don't collect any more taxes than the legal limit. *(The Tax Collector stands.)*

Soldier: *(steps forward and kneels)* What about soldiers? How will this baptism change my life? How am I to repent?

John: *(baptizes the soldier)* Don't take anything by force. Don't accuse people falsely. *(The Soldier stands.)*

Bystander: *(steps forward and kneels)* What about the rest of us?

John: *(baptizes the Bystander)* If you have two shirts in your closet, give one to somebody who has none. If you have food, share it. *(The Bystander stands.)*

Tax Collector: *(as the Pharisees enter from stage left)* Teacher, here come a group of Pharisees. What words do you have for them?

John: *(shakes his fist at the Pharisees, who halt suddenly)* You snakes! Who ever told you that you would escape God's punishment?

1st Pharisee: *(to friend)* This man is out of his mind!

John: Saying that you're children of Abraham isn't good enough! *(points to the ground)* I tell you God can take these stones and make them into children of Abraham!

2nd Pharisee: *(to friend)* He's just as bad as we heard! We'd better report this.

John: Every tree that doesn't bear good fruit will be cut down and thrown into the fire! *(The Pharisees turn and exit stage left. The Levites enter from stage right.)*

1st Levite: *(approaches John timidly)* Teacher, who are you? Are you the Messiah?

John: *(gently but firmly)* I am not. I baptize with water, but someone's coming who will baptize with the Holy Spirit and with fire.

2nd Levite: Who are you then? Are you Elijah or a prophet?

John: I'm a voice shouting in the wilderness, "Prepare the way of the Lord!"

1st Levite: *(to 2nd Levite)* We should take an answer back to those who sent us. This man needs watching.

2nd Levite: *(pauses)* I want to stay and listen. There's something in his preaching that rings true. *(1st Levite exits left. All others exit right, except John who stands center stage.)*

Narrator: Hundreds came to hear John preach and to be baptized in the Jordan. Even Jesus came and was baptized. Then King Herod grew angry because John preached against him for marrying his brother's wife. So he arrested John and threw him in prison. Even in prison, though, John's followers were able to visit and told him what was happening outside.

Messenger: *(enters from stage right)* I took your message to Jesus, the prophet from Nazareth. I asked him if he's the one who is to come, or if we should wait for another.

John: How did he answer you?

Messenger: He said to tell you that the blind can see, the deaf can hear, and the poor have the good news preached to them.

John: *(sighs)* Good. Now I can be at peace. *(John and the Messenger stand motionless as the Narrator reads.)*

Narrator: John the Baptist may have found peace after hearing what Jesus said, but Herod's wife had no peace in her heart. She was constantly looking for ways to get even with John. *(John and the Messenger exit right. Herod and Herodias enter from stage left.)*

Herodias: Your Majesty, I'm glad you put John the Baptist in prison. We couldn't allow him to keep saying that it's not right for me to be married to you.

King Herod: Even though what he says troubles me, I still like to listen to him.

Herodias: You allow him too many visitors. Well, let's not think about it now. Tonight is your birthday feast and we must get ready! *(They move center stage as Salome and their guests enter from stage left.)*

Narrator: No expense was spared for the banquet or for the entertainment. Herod was very pleased and also very drunk.

King Herod: *(drunkenly)* This is the finest celebration I've ever seen! My guests are still talking about your daughter's dance!

Herodias: Come here, Salome! The King wants to thank you for your dancing. *(Salome approaches.)*

King Herod: Your dance was beautiful, my dear. I would like to reward you. Ask me for anything, even half my kingdom, and I will give it to you! *(laughs)*

Salome: *(whispers to her mother)* What shall I ask for?

Herodias: *(whispers her answer)* Ask for the head of John the Baptist!

Salome: *(to the King)* I want you to give me the head of John the Baptist on a silver platter! *(pauses and looks at the King)*

King Herod: *(suddenly sober and sad)* I made a promise to you in front of all my guests. I must do it. *(beckons the Guard)* Guard, go at once and bring back the Baptist's head!

Narrator: When John's friends heard what happened, they came for John's body and buried it. Jesus told them that John the Baptist was the greatest man who ever lived before the coming of the kingdom.

Andrew–Drawing People to Jesus

Narrator: Andrew and his friend John, the son of Zebedee, were followers of John the Baptist. Together they listened to the Baptist preaching on the banks of the River Jordan. *(John Zebedee, Andrew, John the Baptist, and the crowd enter from stage right. John the Baptist crosses to center stage where he begins preaching to the crowd. Andrew and John Zebedee stand apart and watch.)*

John Zebedee: The Baptizer is full of fire today, isn't he, Andrew? It's been like this all week. *(pauses)* Look at the man coming to be baptized now! There's something different about him. *(Jesus enters from stage left.)*

Andrew: I wonder why the Baptist is shaking his head? Doesn't he want to baptize this man? Let's go closer. *(They move closer.)*

John the Baptist: *(to Jesus)* But I'm not worthy to untie the strap of your shoe! I should be baptized by <u>you</u>! Yet here you are, coming to <u>me</u>!

Jesus: Let the baptism be done this way. *(He kneels and John the Baptist pretends to scoop water from the river to baptize Jesus.)*

Andrew: What's happening? A light is coming out of that cloud!

Voice from Heaven: *(from offstage)* This is my beloved Son, with whom I am well pleased.

John Zebedee: *(looks around)* Did you hear that voice? Where did it come from?

Andrew: Could it have been the voice of God? Look at that white dove! How beautiful it is! What does this mean?

John the Baptist: *(points to Jesus)* This is the Lamb of God who takes away the sins of the world!

Andrew: *(to John Zebedee)* Did the Baptist say "Lamb of God"? Is that the man's name?

John the Baptist: *(points to Jesus again)* This is the man I was talking about when I said someone is coming who is greater than I am! I tell you he is the Lamb of God!

John Zebedee: Andrew, what should we do?

Andrew: Let's follow this "Lamb of God" and see what we can find out. *(They move toward Jesus.)*

Jesus: *(turns and looks at them)* What are you doing? What are you looking for?

Andrew: Teacher, where do you live?

Jesus: Come and see. *(turns and crosses to center stage, with Andrew and John Zebedee behind him. The crowd exits left.)*

Narrator: Andrew and John went with Jesus and found out where he lived. Afterward Andrew brought his brother Simon to meet Jesus. *(Andrew crosses to stage left, where Simon enters, carrying a net.)*

Andrew: I tell you, Simon, we've found the Messiah! Wait 'til you see! Come on! *(tugs at Simon's sleeve)*

Simon: Andrew, you're always dragging me away from our fishing nets. I don't see how you can tell from one meeting that this man is the Messiah.

Andrew: You'll see for yourself once you talk to him. *(They walk over to Jesus.)* Here he is.

Jesus: Your name is Simon, son of John, but from now on you will be called Peter. You're a rock, and upon this rock I will build my church. *(All stand motionless as the Narrator reads.)*

Narrator: Peter knew at once what his brother meant about Jesus. He immediately joined the others. Compared to Peter, his famous brother, Andrew stayed in the background, but he was always bringing other people to Jesus. The gospel story of the loaves and fishes is a good example. *(The crowd enters from stage left and stand around Jesus, who is preaching. Philip enters with the crowd and joins Andrew.)*

Philip: *(to Andrew)* Look at the size of the crowd, Andrew! *(points to the crowd)* There must be thousands on this hillside! They've been here all day listening to Jesus.

Andrew: And they haven't had anything to eat yet. It's so hot today! *(wipes his brow)*

Philip: *(looks at the crowd)* We should send them home.

Andrew: *(tugs at Philip's sleeve)* Philip, Jesus is calling for us. *(They go to Jesus.)*

Jesus: Philip, where can we buy food to feed all these people?

Philip: Lord, we don't have money enough to buy even a little bit of bread for this many!

Andrew: Teacher, a little boy over there has five barley loaves and two fish. But what good is that with so many people?

Jesus: Tell everyone to sit down on the grass. Andrew, bring the boy here. *(Philip motions for the crowd to sit.)*

Andrew: *(brings the boy, carrying a basket, to Jesus)* Here he is, Lord. And here's his basket.

Jesus: Thank you, young man. You're good to share your food with us. *(takes the basket and lifts it to heaven)* Blessed be God, King of the Universe, for giving us food to eat. Thank you, Father. *(turning to Andrew and Philip)* Take this and give it to the people. *(Philip and Andrew take the basket and begin to pretend to hand pieces of bread and fish to the crowd.)*

Andrew: *(as he gives out bread and fish)* Philip, the more I give out, the more I have left to give!

Philip: The basket is always full!

Andrew: There's enough bread and fish for everyone! It's a miracle!

Philip: And they all seem to be eating as much as they want!

Andrew: Jesus said to gather all the leftovers so we won't waste anything. We're going to need more baskets. *(goes around gathering up pieces of bread and fish)*

Philip: Let's put the baskets over there. *(Philip and Andrew pretend to arrange the baskets.)*

Andrew: *(counting)* ...nine, ten, eleven, twelve! Philip, we have twelve baskets left over from five barley loaves and two fish! This is a great miracle! We must thank God! *(All stand motionless as the Narrator reads.)*

Narrator: Andrew continued to draw people to Jesus, but we don't hear too much more about him in the Bible. Stories from early Church history, though, tell us that after the resurrection of Jesus, Andrew was one of the founders of the Church in Greece and Turkey and was eventually crucified on an X-shaped cross.

Matthew—Accepting Jesus' Call

Narrator: Matthew, also known as Levi, was a tax collector. In our Lord's time, a tax collector could demand more money than needed from each taxpayer and keep the difference for himself. Tax collectors were not very popular! Devout Jews would not associate with tax collectors because they were agents of Caesar. *(Matthew and an Assistant sit at a table, center stage, with money bags and scrolls. A Farmer enters from the right.)*

Assistant: *(whispers to Matthew)* Here comes another farmer from the hill country, Matthew. The crops were good this year. We'll get extra shekels out of this one.

Farmer: *(slaps coins on table)* Here's my tax for Caesar! Make sure to mark my name down.

Matthew: Good. Let me count it to make sure. *(counts to himself)* You owe me three more shekels.

Farmer: *(angry)* What! How can that be?

Matthew: I say, you owe me three more shekels!

Farmer: *(grumbles and reaches into his money pouch)* All you tax collectors are the same! You squeeze as much money as you can out of us! I'll be glad when the Messiah comes. Then we'll be free of tax collectors. You betray your own people! *(stomps off stage right; Jesus and a friend enter from stage left.)*

Assistant: Weren't you too hard on that man, Matthew? Two extra shekels would have been enough. You didn't need to take three.

Matthew: *(checks his list)* I know. But it really doesn't matter. Everyone hates tax collectors anyway.

Assistant: *(points stage left)* Jesus, the man everybody's talking about, is over there across the street. People are saying he might be the Messiah we've been waiting for.

Matthew: *(looks up from his list, toward Jesus)* He's coming here. I wonder what he wants.

Jesus: *(comes over to table and looks Matthew straight in the eye)* Come. Follow me. *(turns and exits stage left with his friend)*

Matthew: *(stands up)* I'm going to do what he says! There's something about this man!

Assistant: But you can't jump up and go like this!

Matthew: Why not?

Assistant: What about your share of the taxes?

Matthew: Keep it! I'm leaving. *(He hurries after Jesus. The Assistant exits stage right with the money and scrolls.)*

Narrator: This is how Matthew became one of Jesus' first followers. Later, Matthew held a banquet at his house for Jesus, the apostles, and the friends from his old tax collecting job. *(The 1st Tax collector, 2nd Tax Collector, Matthew, and Jesus enter from stage left, carrying goblets. They sit at the table.)*

1st Tax Collector: *(raises his goblet)* What a feast this is, Matthew!

2nd Tax Collector: Thank you for inviting us. It's wonderful to be at a banquet with your new friends.

Matthew: My pleasure. Remember how Jesus says the kingdom of heaven is like a banquet? This is a little taste of what the kingdom is like! *(All laugh.)*

1st Pharisee: (*enters from stage right and angrily addresses Jesus*) How can you be seen with all these tax collectors and public sinners? No self-respecting Jew should be here!

2nd Pharisee: (*points to all the dinner guests*) The Torah forbids sharing a meal with such people!

Jesus: (*calmly*) Those who are well don't need a doctor. Only those people who need healing.

1st Pharisee: What do you mean by that remark?

Jesus: You Pharisees study the Scripture every day. Go and learn what's meant when Scripture says, "It's mercy God wants, not animal sacrifice."

2nd Pharisee: I've known that line by heart for years! You can't tell me anything I don't already know! You still haven't explained why you're breaking bread with tax collectors!

Jesus: I've come to call sinners, not the righteous.

1st Pharisee: (*to 2nd Pharisee*) Come, let's go. He's speaking in riddles. I don't understand this man at all! (*They exit stage right. The others move stage left while stagehands remove the table. Thomas joins the group on the stage.*)

Narrator: The scribes and Pharisees never did understand Jesus. Their hatred helped crucify him. But after Jesus rose from the dead, he appeared many times to Matthew and the other disciples. What follows is just one incident that occurred shortly after the first Easter.

Thomas: (*to Matthew, as group moves to center stage*) Hasn't the last month been amazing, Matthew? When you told me Jesus had risen from the dead, I didn't believe you at first. But the day I touched the wound in his side I was speechless!

Matthew: We've been blessed to hear Jesus preaching the last few weeks. It makes much more sense now. But hush. Let's listen to what he's saying.

Jesus: (*speaks loudly and raises his hands*) I want you to wait for the gift I told you about, the gift my Father promised. John the Baptist baptized with water, but in a few days you'll be baptized with the Holy Spirit.

Thomas: (*to Matthew*) Matthew, do you understand what he's talking about?

Matthew: Shhh. No, I don't. But we always learn what he means later on.

Thomas: (*to Jesus*) Lord, are you going to give the kingdom back to Israel now?

Jesus: The times are set by my Father. It's not for you to know. But when the Holy Spirit comes, you'll be filled with power and you'll be my witnesses to all the world. (*Jesus lifts his arms slowly to signify his ascension into heaven. At the same time, two stagehands standing behind him cover him with a sheet, removing him from sight. All stand motionless.*)

1st Angel: (*enters from stage right*) Men of Galilee, why are you standing here looking up at the sky?

2nd Angel: Jesus, who was taken from your sight, will come back the same way you saw him go up to heaven. (*The angels stand motionless.*)

Thomas: (*shakes his head*) All this is so hard to believe, Matthew! (*pauses*) We'd better go back to Jerusalem as Jesus told us. (*turns to go*)

Matthew: Go on with the others, Thomas. I'll catch up with you. I need to be alone here for a few minutes to pray and think about these things. (*Thomas and the others exit stage left. Matthew kneels.*)

Martha, Mary, and Lazarus—Choosing the Right Thing

Narrator: In Bethany, about a mile and a half from Jerusalem, there was a house Jesus visited often, the home of Lazarus and his two sisters, Martha and Mary. It was a place where Jesus could relax and enjoy the hospitality of good friends. *(Martha, Mary, and Lazarus enter from stage right and cross to a table and chairs upstage center. Lazarus wears a robe to cover the grave wrappings needed for the next scene.)*

Martha: *(wrings her hands)* We still have so much to do! Jesus and his friends will be here any minute.

Lazarus: Settle down, Martha. Dinner will be fine.

Martha: *(points stage left)* Here he comes now! *(Jesus enters with friends.)* Welcome to our house, Lord. Come in! Come in!

Jesus: Martha, Mary, Lazarus! How are you?

Mary: I'm so glad to see you, Lord!

Martha: If everyone will excuse me, I need to go to the kitchen. *(She exits stage right. The others gather around Jesus, and Mary sits at his feet.)*

Mary: Teacher, I love to hear you talk about what the kingdom is like. Can you tell us more?

Martha: *(enters angrily and stands with her hands on her hips)* Lord, don't you care that my sister has left me to do all the work by myself? Tell her to come to the kitchen and help me!

Jesus: Martha, Martha! You're worried about so many things. But really just one thing matters. Mary's chosen the right thing, and it won't be taken away from her. *(Jesus nods to Mary. Martha just stands there, puzzled. After a pause, Lazarus exits stage left. Jesus, his friends, and Mary exit stage right.)*

Narrator: Some time later Lazarus became ill and died. It was a terrible shock to his sisters and the others who loved him. *(1st Relative and 2nd Relative enter stage right and cross to Martha, who is crying.)*

1st Relative: Martha, we're so sorry about Lazarus. Why didn't you send a message to Jesus?

Martha: *(wiping her eyes)* I did, about a week ago. I don't know why he didn't come in time.

2nd Relative: He probably couldn't have done anything anyway. *(points stage right as Jesus and his friends enter)* Look, here he comes now.

Martha: *(runs to Jesus)* If you'd been here, Lord, my brother would not have died. But even now God will give you whatever you ask for.

Jesus: *(takes Martha's hand)* Your brother will rise again.

Martha: *(wipes her tears away and nods her head)* I know he'll rise again on the last day.

Jesus: I am the resurrection and the life. Those who believe in me will live, even though they die. Do you believe this?

Martha: Yes, Lord. I believe you are the Messiah, the Son of God.

Mary: *(enters from stage right, hurries to Jesus, and throws herself at his feet, weeping)* Lord, if you'd been here, my brother wouldn't have died!

Jesus: *(bows his head and wipes away tears)* Where have you buried him?

Martha and Mary: Come and see, Lord. *(They cross to stage left.)*

1st Relative: *(to a companion)* Did you see Jesus' tears? He must have loved Lazarus very much. *(1st Relative and 2nd Relative move stage left to join the others.)*

Martha and Mary: *(points off stage)* The tomb's right there, Lord.

Jesus: *(calls offstage)* Roll the stone away from the entrance.

Martha: *(alarmed)* No, Lord! Don't do that! Lazarus has been dead for four days. There'll be a terrible smell!

Jesus: *(to Martha)* Didn't I say you'd see God's glory if you believed?

Martha: Yes, Lord. *(She looks subdued. Jesus' friends exit stage left.)*

Jesus: *(looks up to heaven)* I thank you, Father, that you listen to me. I say this so the people here will believe you sent me. *(calls in a loud voice)* Lazarus, come out! *(Lazarus slowly walks on stage, wrapped in strips of grave cloth, and followed by Jesus' friends.)*

1st Relative: He's alive! He's walking, even in burial wrappings! It's a miracle!

2nd Relative: *(to himself)* Hmmm. This time Jesus has gone too far.

Jesus: *(calls to his friends)* Unbind him! Let him go! *(Jesus' friends begin to remove Lazarus' grave wrappings.)*

Martha: Lazarus! You're alive!

1st Relative: Jesus really is the Messiah, just as Martha and Mary have been telling us!

2nd Relative: *(to himself)* I better go back and tell the chief priests about this. They're not going to like it. *(exits stage right; others surround Lazarus, then stand motionless as the Narrator reads.)*

Narrator: About a week before Jesus died, he was once again at Bethany with his friends. *(All move to the table. Judas joins them. Lazarus wears a robe to cover any remaining grave wrappings. Martha and Mary exit stage right.)*

Peter: *(raises his goblet)* Good choice of wine, Lazarus!

Lazarus: Martha is the one who bought it. She takes care of all the details.

Peter: Have you heard how many more people have been coming to hear Jesus since the miracle he performed for you? We can't go anywhere in peace these days! *(Mary enters from stage right, carrying a jar of perfume.)*

Judas: What's Mary doing now? It looks like she has a jar of perfume. *(Mary pretends to be pouring perfume on Jesus' feet.)* Now she's pouring it all over Jesus' feet!

Peter: The sweet smell of it is filling the whole house! *(Mary wipes Jesus' feet with her hair.)*

Judas: Perfume is too expensive to waste like that! She could have sold it for 300 pieces of silver. She could have given the money to the poor instead of pouring it all away!

Jesus: Judas, leave her alone! She has anointed me for the day of my burial. You'll always have poor people with you, but you won't always have me. *(All pause and stand motionless for a minute.)*

John the Evangelist— Following Jesus to the Cross

Narrator: John, the author of the fourth gospel, was the son of Zebedee, a fisherman. He and his brother James were part of Jesus' inner circle of friends. In this scene John and James are walking up Mount Tabor, following Jesus and Peter.

James: *(lags behind Jesus as all enter from stage right)* John, how much farther up the mountain do you think Jesus is taking us?

John: To the top, it looks like. He must want a quiet place to pray. *(They cross to center stage.)* Did you understand what he told us last month about drinking a cup of suffering? You know, when we asked if we could sit at his right hand in the kingdom?

James: No, I still don't understand it. *(pauses)* Here we are at the top. I wonder why he brought only three of us and left the others behind.

Peter: *(to John, as Jesus crosses alone to upstage center)* I'm tired! I need to sit down!

John: Not now, Peter! Look at Jesus' face! Look at his clothes! They're bright as the sun! *(Two figures in white enter from stage left and stand beside Jesus.)*

James: Where did those two come from? Who are they? One looks like Moses!

John: I think the other's Elijah! *(They fall silent, gazing at Jesus and the two figures in white.)*

Peter: *(excited)* Lord, it's good to be here! Let's set up three tents—one for you, one for Moses, one for Elijah!

John: Peter, we'd better be quiet! Look at that strange cloud! *(pauses)*

Voice of God: *(from offstage)* This is my beloved Son with whom I am pleased. Listen to him! *(Peter, James, and John fall face down, terrified.)*

James: Oh, no! That was God's voice! We're all going to die! *(The two figures in white exit stage left.)*

Jesus: *(crosses the stage, reaches down, and touches Peter)* Don't be afraid! Stand up now. *(The three disciples get up.)*

John: *(looks around)* Are Moses and Elijah gone?

Jesus: Don't tell people about this vision until the Son of Man has been raised from the dead. *(Jesus exits stage right.)*

John: *(The disciples brush themselves off and follow.)* What does he mean by "raised from the dead"?

Peter: I never know what he means. But hurry. Let's go quickly so we don't miss anything. *(Peter, James, and John exit stage right.)*

Narrator: This event was called the transfiguration. The three friends of Jesus didn't understand it for a long time. But they were also the only witnesses at other key times in the Lord's ministry.

James: *(A crowd, including James and John, enter from stage right and surround Jesus. James and John stand apart.)* John, will you look at this crowd! Where do they all come from?

John: Word keeps spreading. *(Jairus enters from stage left.)* Look, there's the leader of the synagogue. He's pushing his way through to Jesus. He looks so worried!

James: It's the man they call Jairus. Let's help him. *(They cross to Jairus, take his elbow, and bring him to Jesus.)*

Jairus: Lord! My little girl is very sick! Please come and lay your hands on her so she'll get well! *(Jesus reaches out to him but then turns as someone else touches him.)*

John: There are too many people here. It'll be hard for Jesus to leave.

Messenger: *(approaches Jairus from stage left)* Sir, I'm sorry to tell you, but your daughter has died. It's no use to bother the Master any longer.

Jesus: *(touches Jairus)* Don't be afraid. Just believe. *(turns to Peter, James, and John)* Come with me. *(They move stage left.)*

Mother: *(enters from left, weeping)* What can the Teacher do now? She's dead! My only child is dead!

Jesus: She's not dead. She's only sleeping. *(With Peter, James, and John blocking him from view, Jesus walks to stage left, calling in a loud voice.)* Little girl, get up!

Child: *(enters from stage left; the others make way for her. She walks slowly, rubbing her eyes.)* Where am I?

Jairus: *(amazed)* How can this be?

Mother: My little girl! Back from the dead! *(hugs the child)*

Jesus: John, go get the child something to eat.

John: Yes, Lord. I'll go at once. *(Everyone exits.)*

Narrator: Of all the apostles, John was the only one present with Jesus when he died on the cross. The others all ran away. *(Jesus stands stage right in crucified position, with John and Jesus' mother, Mary, at his side. Four Roman soldiers are center stage, talking.)*

1st Soldier: Well, our job's almost finished. These criminals will be dead in a few hours.

2nd Soldier: Yes, we may as well divide up the clothes. *(He shakes out Jesus' tunic)* Look at this. It's woven all in one piece!

3rd Soldier: One of the weavers in Galilee must have made it.

John: *(comforts Mary)* Now, now, Mary.

1st Soldier: *(turns the tunic over)* It's a shame to tear this. Let's throw dice to see who gets it.

2nd, 3rd, and 4th Soldiers: Good idea! *(They throw dice.)*

3rd Soldier: Aha! I win! *(All laugh, then go stand guard at the four corners of the stage.)*

John: *(still comforting Mary)* I know it's hard to be here, but I keep hoping we can do some small thing for him, even now.

Jesus: *(from the cross)* I'm thirsty!

John: *(calls to the 2nd Soldier)* He says he's thirsty! Can you give him something to drink?

2nd Soldier: All we have is cheap wine. *(picks up a cup)*

Jesus: My God, my God, why have you abandoned me?

2nd Soldier: *(puts a sponge soaked in wine on a stick and holds it up to Jesus)* Here, drink this. *(Jesus turns his head away.)*

Jesus: *(pauses, then turns to Mary)* Mother, this is your son. *(He nods at John.)* Son, this is your mother.

John: *(gently draws Mary's head to his shoulder)* Mary, he wants me to take care of you from now on.

Jesus: *(cries out from the cross)* It is finished! *(Jesus' head droops to his chest and he dies. John and Mary kneel.)*

4th Soldier: *(slowly kneels as other soldiers stand guard)* Truly this was the Son of God! *(All stand motionless and the scene ends in this tableau.)*

Mary Magdalene–Proclaiming the Good News

Narrator: Mary Magdalene is known as one of Jesus' most faithful followers. She was one of the very few who followed him all the way to Calvary. *(John the Evangelist, Mary Magdalene, Jesus, Mary [Jesus' mother], Mary [Jesus' mother's sister], 1st Thief, 2nd Thief, 1st Soldier, and 2nd Soldier enter from stage left. Jesus and the thieves go to center stage and stand in crucified position. John and Magdalene are at Jesus' right, Jesus' mother and the other Mary on his left.)*

John: *(looks at the sky)* The sky's been dark for hours, Mary.

Magdalene: I know. It's like the whole earth is sad because of what they've done to Jesus.

1st Passerby: *(enters stage right with companion, crosses to center stage, and shakes a fist at Jesus)* Ha! You said you could tear the temple down and build it back up in three days! Just look at you now! *(pretends to spit and then exits stage left with companion)*

Magdalene: *(to John)* How can people say such things? They're so cruel! Why doesn't God <u>do</u> something?

Jesus: *(looks up to heaven)* Father, forgive them. They don't know what they're doing.

John: Lord, how can you forgive the terrible pain they're causing you to suffer! *(puts his head in his hands)*

1st Thief: *(mocks Jesus)* If you're supposed to be the great Messiah, why don't you save yourself <u>and</u> us! *(laughs mockingly)*

2nd Thief: Don't mock him! We're here because we deserve it, but he hasn't done anything wrong!

Magdalene: *(to John)* The only one here who has any respect for Jesus is this thief!

2nd Thief: *(to Jesus)* Jesus, remember me when you come into your kingdom!

Jesus: *(to the thief)* I tell you, today you will be with me in paradise!

Magdalene: *(to John)* John, Jesus is still loving and forgiving people, even on the cross! How can everyone not recognize him for who he is? *(John puts his arm around Magdalene as she weeps.)*

2nd Passerby: *(enters from stage right with 3rd Passerby)* Look! Let's see if he's really the Son of God! Let's see if he can save himself.

3rd Passerby: *(laughs)* Yes, let's watch him come down from the cross. Then we'll believe! *(They laugh and exit stage left.)*

Jesus: *(looks to heaven)* Father, into your hands I entrust my spirit! *(As he dies, Jesus' head falls onto his chest. His followers kneel.)*

1st Soldier: *(goes over and looks at Jesus, and then says to 2nd Soldier)* Well, we won't have to break this one's legs. He's dead already.

Joseph of Arimathea: *(enters hurriedly from stage right, holding a folded sheet)* John, what's happening?

Magdalene: *(stands up weeping and touches John's shoulder)* John, here's Joseph of Arimathea. It looks like he has brought a burial cloth.

Joseph: *(crosses to embrace Jesus' mother)* I asked Pilate for permission to give Jesus a proper burial. He said yes because he wants everything finished by sundown.

Magdalene: *(weeps)* Where will you bury him?

Joseph: In my own tomb. I had one cut for myself from solid rock. Come. Let's get Nicodemus to help us take Jesus' body down. *(They exit stage right, leaving the crucified figures, Jesus' mother, the other Mary, and the soldiers on the stage. After a long pause, these actors also exit quickly stage right.)*

Narrator: Jesus was buried and a large stone was rolled in front of the tomb. The next day was the Sabbath when no one was permitted to anoint the dead. But very early the following morning Mary Magdalene went to the tomb.

Magdalene: *(enters from stage right, carrying a jar of spices. Peter and John enter with her. She points left, offstage.)* See, Peter! It's just as I told you. I came here early with more spices, and the stone was rolled away!

Peter: *(as they cross the stage)* I see it! I didn't believe you at first! I'm sorry.

John: Someone took Jesus' body! Now we don't know where they put him!

Peter: John, I'm going inside the tomb to see for myself! *(exits stage left)*

John: Me, too! *(follows Peter)*

Magdalene: Be careful!

Peter: *(reenters carrying strips of white cloth)* Look, here are the strips of linen that wrapped his head!

John: *(follows Peter)* What could've happened?

Magdalene: *(weeps)* Who would take Jesus' body?

Peter: *(sighs)* He had so many enemies.

John: We'd better go back home and see what we can find out.

Peter: I'll go with you, John. *(turns to Magdalene)* Mary, we have to go back and tell the others. *(He pats Magdalene on the shoulder, then exits stage right with John.)*

Magdalene: *(covers her eyes)* What am I going to do? Where have they taken him?

Gardener/Jesus: *(enters from stage left)* Peace be with you!

Magdalene: Who are you, Sir?

Gardener/Jesus: Why are you crying? Who are you looking for?

Magdalene: *(wipes her eyes)* Sir, if you took the body of my Lord, tell me where you put him!

Gardener/Jesus: *(looks at her tenderly)* Mary!

Magdalene: Teacher! *(She recognizes Jesus and reaches out to touch his robe.)*

Gardener/Jesus: Don't hold on to me. I haven't gone back yet to the Father. Don't be afraid.

Magdalene: Yes, Lord!

Gardener/Jesus: Go to my friends and tell them that I said, "I'm going to my Father and your Father, to my God and your God."

Magdalene: Yes, Teacher!

Gardener/Jesus: Tell them to go to Galilee and there they will see me.

Magdalene: Teacher, I'll go at once! *(Jesus stands motionless as Magdalene exits hurriedly, stage right.)*

Narrator: Mary Magdalene did as Jesus told her. She was the first person to report the good news of the resurrection.

Peter—Receiving the Strength of the Spirit

Narrator: Since Peter was a fisherman, the Gospels often show him near the sea. *(James, John, and Peter enter, move to center stage, and sit on the floor, leaning first one way and then the other, pretending to be in a boat.)*

James: Peter, we're all going to drown! Surely the boat will overturn any minute!

Peter: I've never seen a wind like this! Or such high waves!

James: Where's Jesus when we need him? It's so dark!

Peter: If only the wind would stop! *(Jesus enters from stage left.)*

James: Peter, look over there! What's that glow?

Peter: It must be from the storm.

John: No, it's a glowing light, and it's moving this way!

Peter: It's shaped like a man. But it can't be, way out here on the water!

James and John: It's a ghost! It's a ghost!

Jesus: Don't be afraid! It's me!

Peter: Lord, *(hesitates a moment and then continues)*, if it's really you, order me to step out on the water and come to you!

Jesus: *(beckons)* Come!

Peter: I will! *(steps out of boat, begins to walk, looks down, and starts to sink)* Save me, Lord! Save me!

Jesus: *(reaches out, takes Peter's hand, and lifts him up)* Peter, Peter! I've called you the rock on which I will build my church! What little faith you have! Why did you doubt? *(They climb into the boat. All stop leaning back and forth. The storm has ended.)*

All: *(look around in awe)* Truly, Lord, you're the Son of God! Thank you for being here! *(All remain motionless for a minute and the scene ends in this tableau. Before the next scene begins, the stagehands move a table and chairs center stage.)*

Narrator: Nowhere in the Gospels do we see Peter's impulsiveness more than on the night of the Last Supper and Jesus' agony in the garden. *(The apostles sit and stand around Jesus at the table. John, Peter, and James are on Jesus' right.)*

James: *(lifts his goblet)* Peter, this is the best Passover we've ever had! You did a fine job. But, wait! Jesus is starting to say something.

Jesus: *(looks at them seriously)* I tell you, one of you here will betray me.

All: *(at the same time, sounding confused)* You don't mean me, do you, Lord?

Peter: *(is upset and whispers to John)* Ask him who he's talking about!

John: *(turns to Jesus)* Lord, who is it who's going to betray you?

Jesus: The one to whom I give this bread dipped in sauce. *(Jesus hands a piece of bread to Judas, who pauses and then runs offstage.)*

James: *(to John)* Jesus can't mean it. None of us would betray him!

Jesus: I have wanted so much to eat this Passover meal with you. *(Jesus takes bread, looks up to heaven, and breaks the bread.)* Take this and eat it—this is my body.

James: *(to Peter)* Did he say his "body"?

Jesus: *(takes a cup and looks up to heaven)* Take this cup and drink it. This is my blood, poured out for the forgiveness of sins.

James: *(to Peter)* He didn't say "blood," did he? We're Jews! We're forbidden to eat anything that has blood in it!

Jesus: Tonight all of you will run away and leave me alone.

Peter: Jesus, I'll never leave you! Even if everyone else does!

Jesus: Peter, before the rooster crows, you'll say you don't even know me.

Peter: Never! I'll never do anything like that! Not even if they threaten to kill me!

Jesus: Hand me that towel, please. *(Jesus gets up from the table, picks up the basin, tucks the towel into his belt, and prepares to wash Peter's feet.)*

Peter: *(jumps up)* No, Lord! You're not going to wash my feet!

Jesus: Peter, you don't understand what I'm doing now, but later on you will.

Peter: No! I won't let you wash my feet!

Jesus: Peter, Peter! If I don't wash your feet, you won't be my disciple any more.

Peter: *(is puzzled and frowns)* All right, then! You can wash my feet and my hands and my head!

Jesus: *(pretends to wash the feet of all of the apostles and then stands up)* Do you understand what I just did? I gave you an example. You must serve each other. *(pauses and then speaks)* Sit here while I go to pray. Peter, James, John—come keep watch with me. *(Jesus leads them stage right. They sit while he kneels and covers his face with his hands.)*

Peter: *(yawns and talks to James and John)* I'm so sleepy! It's been a long day. *(They fall asleep.)*

Jesus: *(looks to heaven)* Father, if possible, take this cup from me. *(sighs, gets up, and goes to Peter and wakes him)* Peter! Can't you watch with me for even one hour! Pray that you don't fall into temptation!

Peter: *(sleepily rubs his eyes)* Yes, Lord. *(Jesus goes back and kneels. Peter falls asleep again.)*

Jesus: *(sighs and wipes his brow)* Father, let your will, not mine, be done. *(gets up, goes back to Peter, James, and John)* Wake up! The hour has come! *(They are startled and stand up.)*

Judas: *(enters from stage left with soldiers)* The man I kiss is the one you want. Arrest him! *(crosses to Jesus and kisses Jesus on cheek. The soldiers move toward Jesus.)*

Peter: *(pulls out his sword and grabs a soldier's sleeve)* Let Jesus go! I'll chop off your ear if you dare touch him! *(The soldier claps one hand over his ear.)*

Jesus: Put your sword away, Peter. *(The soldiers and Judas march Jesus offstage, moving stage right.)*

All: (fearful) We'd better get out of here before they arrest us, too! (They exit hurriedly, stage left. Peter pauses, then starts after Jesus.)

Narrator: Peter followed as the soldiers took Jesus to the high priest. Peter waited outside in the courtyard.

1st Servant Girl: (enters from stage left and points to Peter) I recognize you! You were with Jesus!

Peter: Woman, I don't know what you're talking about! (crosses to center; 1st Servant Girl exits stage left.)

2nd Servant Girl: (enters from stage right with the Manservant) Hey! He was with Jesus of Nazareth!

Peter: I swear I don't know him!

Manservant: Of course you do! I saw you with him in the garden. Besides, I can tell from your accent that you're from Galilee!

Peter: Listen, I swear I'm telling the truth! I don't know the man! (A rooster crows. Peter buries his face in his hands and runs offstage, stage left. The others exit stage right.)

Narrator: After the resurrection Peter became the true leader he was meant to be. The Holy Spirit's power at Pentecost gave him strength. (The apostles enter from stage right and kneel. Peter and Thomas enter from stage left and stand downstage center.)

Peter: (to Thomas) I'm glad Jesus told us to stay together until the Holy Spirit comes.

Thomas: There are over a hundred of us now, Peter! I wonder what will happen next!

Peter: Right now it sounds like a storm is coming. The wind is roaring out there!

Thomas: It's shaking the whole house! What a noise! And so sudden!

Peter: Thomas, watch out! The top of your head's on fire!

Thomas: (touches the top of his head) Yours is, too!

Peter: The others all have tongues of fire, too! Look at them! I feel like I'm being filled to overflowing with strength!

Thomas: This is what Jesus talked about. It's the power of the Holy Spirit!

Peter: I'm bursting to tell the news of what Jesus did for us! (turns to the others) Everybody, let's go outside and tell people about this! (They cross stage left. Pilgrims enter.)

All Apostles: Listen, everyone! Listen to what we have to say! (Pilgrims gasp.)

1st Pilgrim: What's all the excitement? Who are those people?

2nd Pilgrim: They're followers of Jesus of Nazareth, the one who was crucified.

Pilgrims from Egypt: We hear them speaking our own language!

Pilgrims from Mesopotamia: We hear them talking in ours!

Pilgrims from Crete: And ours, too!

All Pilgrims: We all hear them speaking different languages! What does this mean?

1st Pilgrim: What it means is that these people are drunk!

Peter: *(gestures to calm the crowd)* Listen, everyone! We're not drunk. It's only nine o'clock in the morning!

1st Pilgrim: Who's he?

Peter: *(speaks loudly)* All of you, listen! God performed miracles through Jesus of Nazareth and raised him from the dead! We're his witnesses. What you see and hear now is the gift of the Holy Spirit!

2nd Pilgrim: What does this mean for us?

Peter: Turn away from wrongdoing and be baptized in the name of Jesus! Then you'll receive God's gift of the Holy Spirit.

1st Pilgrim: I'm going to do what he says. I want this baptism he's talking about! *(All pause motionless and the scene ends in this tableau.)*

Narrator: Peter led the apostles from then on. Tradition tells us that he followed Christ even to the point of being crucified. But because he didn't think he was worthy to die the same death as the Lord, he asked to be crucified upside down.

Paul–Spreading the Good News

Narrator: Paul, the author of thirteen letters in the New Testament, was not one of the original apostles. In fact, he was a Pharisee known as Saul, who persecuted the apostles. *(Saul and two companions enter from stage left, pretending to be riding horses.)*

1st Companion: *(to companion)* What's the hurry? Why is Saul angry?

2nd Companion: He has letters from Jerusalem. He wants to arrest everyone who follows the new way of Jesus of Nazareth. He hates Jesus' followers.

1st Companion: *(as Saul falls to ground)* Look! He's fallen off his horse!

2nd Companion: *(shields his eyes)* What's that light? It's almost blinding me!

Voice of Jesus: *(from offstage)* Saul! Saul! Why do you persecute me?

Saul: *(looks around)* Who are you, Lord?

Voice of Jesus: I am Jesus of Nazareth, whom you persecute. Get up now and go to Damascus. You'll be told what to do.

1st Companion: What was that voice? Where did it come from?

2nd Companion: *(Saul gets up, but stumbles.)* Saul is stumbling around! The light must have blinded him! *(His companions take Saul by the hand, lead him stage right, and then exit.)*

Narrator: Saul's friends led him to the city. He remained blind for three days. But then a disciple of the Lord came to see him.

Ananias: *(enters from stage left)* Brother Saul, the Lord Jesus sent me a vision. He told me to lay hands on you so you could see again. I know you've been persecuting us, but here I am. *(He crosses the stage and lays his hands over Saul's eyes.)*

Saul: *(Amazed, Saul pauses, blinks, and looks around.)* It's as if scales have fallen from my eyes! I'm not blind any more! Thanks be to God!

Ananias: God chose you to tell people what you've seen and heard. Now, stand up and be baptized. Let your sins be washed away by praying to him.

Saul: *(bows his head)* This is what I want! *(Ananias baptizes him.)*

Narrator: After his conversion, Saul was called Paul and traveled from city to city all around the Mediterranean, telling people about Jesus and founding Christian communities. Often Paul was beaten, almost stoned to death, and thrown in prison. *(Ananias exits while the Jailer and Silas enter from stage right. Paul sits on the floor.)*

Jailer: *(to Paul)* You're lucky they didn't do more than just whip you! I've got my orders to lock you up tight. They say you can work miracles. *(shoves Silas down next to Paul)*

Silas: They came for me, too, Paul.

Jailer: *(to Paul and Silas)* Put your feet in front of you so I can chain them. You won't see any miracles tonight! *(wraps chain loosely around the prisoners' feet and exits stage right)*

Paul: Silas, are you all right? Those whippings are harsh. People take offense at our preaching and then this is what happens.

Silas: I know. But you wrote in your last letter that we have to preach the good news whether it's welcome or unwelcome.

Paul: Let's pray and sing a few hymns. It'll take our minds off our troubles and give glory to God.

Silas: *(lurches from side to side)* Paul! I think it's an earthquake! The ground is rumbling! Look! The door to the prison is swinging open! Our chains are falling off! *(They pull the chains off, stand, and cross to stage left.)*

Jailer: *(rushes onstage)* What's happening? If my prisoners escape, the Romans will have my head! I'll kill myself before I let them kill me! *(pulls out his sword)*

Paul: Stop! Don't harm yourself! We're over here!

Jailer: What? You didn't escape! *(pauses)* Is the Messiah truly who you say he is? *(pauses)* What must I do to be saved?

Paul: Believe in the Lord Jesus, and you and your whole family will be saved.

Jailer: Let me light some torches. I'll take you home and dress your wounds. I want you to baptize my wife and children and my servants, too. *(All exit stage left.)*

Narrator: Paul made three incredible missionary journeys. Among his first companions was Mark. Later, he traveled with Luke. Always there was hardship. At last Paul was arrested and sent to Rome to stand trial as a Roman citizen. On the way, a violent storm washed his ship off course. *(The Sailor, Roman Guard, Paul, and Luke enter from stage left, shivering. They cross to center stage, where the Island Chieftain is building a fire.)*

Sailor: Here we are, shipwrecked! Why didn't you let me throw the prisoners overboard during that storm? They've brought us nothing but bad luck.

Roman Guard: I can't let you kill them. The one named Paul is a Roman citizen and must have a trial before the emperor. I want to get him safely to Rome.

Sailor: Then all of us are doomed! It's freezing cold and our ship is lost. What's the name of this island, anyway?

Paul: Come closer to the fire, Sailor. Luke, help me gather more wood.

Luke: *(to the Island Chieftain, while handing Paul a bundle of wood)* How good it was of you to get this fire started for us.

Roman Guard: Watch out, Paul! There's a snake crawling out of the wood!

Sailor: It's poisonous! It's biting the prisoner's hand! I told you he's doomed! *(Paul shakes his hand.)*

Luke: No, he's shaking the creature off into the fire. The Lord has more work for his servant Paul to do.

Island Chieftain: *(to Paul)* Why didn't you die? Are you a god? Will you come to my house and cure my father? He's very sick.

Paul: No, I'm not a god. There's only one God, who is in heaven. But I'll pray and lay hands on your father and, with God's grace, he'll be healed. Come, Luke! Let's go to the house of this good man. *(They exit stage right.)*

Narrator: For the rest of the winter, Paul and Luke remained on the island. In the spring, they set sail once again. In Rome Paul was under house arrest for two years. His friends were able to visit him freely, and he preached and wrote many letters during this time. Paul was finally beheaded about 67 AD.

Notes for the Director

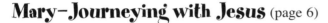

Mary–Journeying with Jesus (page 6)

Cast: Narrator, Joseph, Mary, Simeon, Anna, 1st Wise Man, 2nd Wise Man, 3rd Wise Man, Jesus, Philip, Nathaniel, Worried Servant, Wine Steward, Groom, 1st Servant, 2nd Servant (non-speaking parts: men and women traveling from Jerusalem, wedding guests)

Scenes: temple, Bethlehem, Jerusalem, Cana

Props: large baby doll wrapped in a blanket • cane for Anna • gifts for the wise men to carry • plastic wine glasses, drinking glasses, or paper cups for goblets • six large containers for water jars

Key Words and Pronunciations:
Astrologers—Those who study the stars
Cana (KAY-nuh)—A town in Galilee
Flight into Egypt—The holy family's escape from King Herod
Herod—The powerful King of Judea
Nathaniel—An apostle
Nazareth—A village in Galilee
Philip—An apostle
Rabbi—A teacher
Simeon (SIM-ee-un)—An old man in the temple
Temple—The central place of worship in Jerusalem

Scripture: Luke 1:26-38 • Luke 2:22-38 • Matthew 2:1-12 • Luke 2:41-51 • John 2:1-12

Elizabeth–Believing and Praising God

(page 9)

Cast: Narrator, Elizabeth, Maidservant, 1st Priest, 2nd Priest, Zechariah, Mary, Neighbor, Midwife, Relative

Scenes: Zechariah's house

Props: magic slate for the wax tablet • baby doll wrapped in a blanket

Key Words and Pronunciations:
Abraham—The father in faith of the Jews
Annunciation—Gabriel's announcement that Mary will be the mother of the son of God
Circumcision—The removal of the foreskin of the male sex organ
Covenant—The solemn agreement made between God and the Israelites

Elijah (uh-LYE-juh)—An Old Testament prophet
Elizabeth—Mary's cousin, the mother of John the Baptist
Gabriel—An archangel, a messenger of God
Visitation—The visit Mary made to Elizabeth after the annunciation
Zechariah (zek-uh-RYE-uh)—Elizabeth's husband, the father of John the Baptist

Scripture: Luke 1:5-66

John the Baptist– Preparing the Way for Jesus (page 11)

Cast: Narrator, Soldier, Tax Collector, Bystander, John the Baptist, 1st Pharisee, 2nd Pharisee, 1st Levite, 2nd Levite, Messenger, Herodias, Herod, Salome (non-speaking parts: party guests, Guard)

Scenes: River Jordan, prison, Herod's palace

Props: leather or fleece vest for John the Baptist • cup or shell for baptizing • plastic wine glasses, drinking glasses, or paper cups for goblets

Key Words and Pronuncations:
Elijah (uh-LYE-juh)—An Old Testament prophet
Herod—A ruler, but not the same one who threatened the life of Jesus
Herodias (huh-ROH-dee-us)—The wife of Herod
Jordan—A river on the Promised Land's eastern edge
Levite (LEE-vite)—An official who serves in the temple
Messiah—The "anointed one" who was expected to save Israel
Pharisees (FAIR-uh-sees)—Jews who observed the law very strictly
Prophet—One who speaks the word of God
Salome (suh-LOH-mee or SAL-oh-may)—The daughter of Herodias

Scripture: Luke 3:1-20 • Matthew 14:1-12

Andrew–Drawing People to Jesus

(page 13)

Cast: Narrator, John Zebedee, Andrew, John the Baptist, Jesus, Voice from Heaven, Simon/Peter, Philip (non-speaking parts: crowd, a little boy)

Scenes: River Jordan, Sea of Galilee, hillside

Props: leather or fleece vest for John the Baptist • cup or shell for baptizing • fishing net • several large baskets

Key Words and Pronunciations:
Barley—A grain that was the food of the poor
Jordan—A river on the promised land's eastern edge
Messiah—The "anointed one" who was expected to save Israel
Philip—An apostle
Resurrection—Jesus' rising from the dead
Simon—Andrew's brother who became known as the apostle Peter
Zebedee (ZEB-uh-dee)—A fisherman of Galilee

Scripture: Mark 1:16-20 • John 1:26-34 • John 6:1-14

Matthew—Accepting Jesus' Call (page 15)

Cast: Narrator, Assistant, Matthew, Farmer, Jesus, 1st Tax Collector, 2nd Tax Collector, 1st Pharisee, 2nd Pharisee, Thomas, 1st Angel, 2nd Angel (non-speaking parts: Jesus' friend, two stagehands)

Scenes: tax booth, Matthew's house, Mount of Olives

Props: table and chairs • rolls of shelf paper for scrolls • brown bags stuffed with crumpled paper and labeled with dollar signs for money bags • play money or poker chips for coins • plastic wine glasses, drinking glasses, or paper cups for goblets • a white bedsheet

Key Words and Pronunciations:
Caesar—The Roman emperor
Levi—Another name for Matthew
Pharisees (FAIR-uh-sees)—Jews who observed the law very strictly
Scribes—Scholars, experts on the law
Shekel (SHEK-ul)—A coin
Tax collector—One who collected taxes or tolls
Torah—The written collection of the law, the first five books of the Bible, also called the Pentateuch

Scripture: Matthew 9:9-13 • Acts 1:6-11

Martha, Mary, and Lazarus—Choosing the Right Thing (page 17)

Cast: Narrator, Martha, Lazarus, Jesus, Mary (who should have long hair), 1st Relative, 2nd Relative, Peter, Judas (non-speaking parts: Jesus' friends)

Scenes: inside Lazarus' house, outside Lazarus' tomb

Props: table and chairs • plastic wine glasses, drinking glasses, or paper cups for goblets • a robe for Lazarus to wear over his burial wrappings • strips of paper or cloth for burial wrappings (toilet paper is ideal) • a container for the jar of perfume

Key Words and Pronunciations:
Bethany (BETH-uh-nee)—A village near the Mount of Olives
Jerusalem—The capital city of Judea
Judas—The apostle who betrayed Jesus
Lazarus—The brother of Martha and Mary
Messiah—The "anointed one" who was expected to save Israel
Resurrection—Jesus' rising from the dead

Scripture: Luke 10:38-42 • John 11:1-44 • John 12:1-8

John the Evangelist—Following Jesus to the Cross (page 19)

Cast: Narrator, James, John, Peter, Voice of God, Jesus, Jairus, Messenger, Mother, Child, 1st Soldier, 2nd Soldier, 3rd Soldier, 4th Soldier (non-speaking parts: Elijah, Moses, Mary, crowd)

Scenes: Mount Tabor, outside Jairus' house, Calvary

Props: white fabric for tunics for Moses and Elijah • T-shirt for Jesus' seamless tunic • dice • cup • wine jug • sponge • stick

Key Words and Pronunciations:
Elijah (uh-LYE-juh)—An Old Testament prophet
Galilee—A region of the holy land north of Jerusalem
Jairus (JYE-rus)—An official at the synagogue
Moses—The Old Testament prophet who led the Israelites out of Egypt
Mount Tabor—A mountain east of Nazareth
Synagogue (SIHN-uh-gog)—A Jewish place of worship and learning
Transfiguration—Jesus' changed appearance on Mount Tabor
Zebedee (ZEB-uh-dee)—A fisherman of Galilee

Scripture: Matthew 17:1-9 • Mark 5:21-24, 35-43 • John 19:16-30 • Matthew 27:54

Mary Magdalene—Proclaiming the Good News (page 22)

Cast: Narrator, John the Evangelist, Mary Magdalene, 1st Passerby, Jesus (who also plays Gardener/Jesus), 1st Thief, 2nd Thief, 2nd Passerby, 3rd Passerby, 1st Soldier, Joseph of Arimathea, Peter (non-speaking parts: 1st Passerby's companion, Mary [Jesus' mother], Mary [Jesus' mother's sister], 2nd Soldier)

Scenes: Calvary, area just outside the tomb

Props: A folded white bedsheet • strips of white cloth or paper for burial wrapping (toilet paper is ideal) • jar of potpourri for the spices

Key Words and Pronunciations:
Calvary—The place where Jesus was crucified
Evangelist—One who announces good news
Gardener—Jesus, in his appearance to Mary Magdalene after the resurrection
Joseph of Arimathea (ar-uh-muh-THEE-un)—A wealthy member of the Jewish council
Nicodemus (nik-uh-DEE-muss)—A member of the Jewish council
Resurrection—Jesus' rising from the dead
Sabbath—A day set for rest and religious activity
Spices—Fragrances used for anointing and embalming the dead

Scripture: John 19:16-42 • John 20:14-18

Peter—Receiving the Strength of the Spirit (page 24)

Cast: Narrator, James, Peter, John, Jesus, Judas, Eight Other Apostles, 1st Servant Girl, 2nd Servant Girl, Manservant, Thomas, 1st Pilgrim, 2nd Pilgrim, Pilgrims from Egypt, Pilgrims from Mesopotamia, Pilgrims from Crete (non-speaking parts: two stagehands, soldiers)

Scenes: Sea of Galilee, the upper room, courtyard of the high priest

Props: table and chairs • plastic wine glasses, drinking glasses, or paper cups for goblets • a loaf of unsliced bread • towel • basin • sword for Peter • signs for the pilgrims to wear, "Pilgrim from Egypt," "Pilgrim from Mesopotamia," and "Pilgrim from Crete"

Key Words and Pronunciations:
Agony in the garden—Jesus' prayerful struggle before he was arrested
Betray—To deliver someone over to an enemy
Crete—A Greek island
Denial—Saying something is not true
Egypt—A country in Africa
Judas—The apostle who betrayed Jesus
Last Supper—The last meal Jesus shared with his apostles
Mesopotamia (mess-uh-puh-TAY-mee-uh)—The land between the Tigris and the Euphrates Rivers
Passover—The annual Jewish celebration of their escape from Egypt

Pentecost—The celebration of the coming of the Holy Spirit to the apostles and the beginning of the Church
Pilgrims—Those who travel somewhere for religious reasons
Rock—A pun in Greek on the apostle Peter's name
Rooster—A symbol of Peter's denial of Jesus

Scripture: Matthew 14: 22-33 • Mark 14:12-50 • Acts 2:1-21 • Acts 2:37-39

Paul—Spreading the Good News (page 28)

Cast: Narrator, 1st Companion, 2nd Companion, Voice of Jesus, Saul/Paul, Ananias, Jailer, Silas, Sailor, Roman guard, Luke, Island Chieftain

Scenes: road to Damascus, jail, the island of Malta

Props: cup or shell for baptizing • two short lengths of light chain such as that used to chain a dog • bundle of firewood or sticks • plastic snake

Key Words and Pronunciations:
Ananias (an-uh-NYE-us)—An early Christian
Conversion—A change from one viewpoint to another
Damascus (duh-MASS-cuss)—An ancient city and capitol of modern Syria
Mediterranean—The sea surrounded by Africa, Europe, and Asia
Messiah—The "anointed one" who was expected to save Israel
Persecute—To harass a group because of their beliefs
Pharisees (FAIR-uh-sees)—Jews who observed the law very strictly
Saul—Paul's name before his conversion
Silas—A companion of Paul

Scripture: Acts 9:1-19 • Acts 16:16-34 • Acts 27:39-28:10

Post-Skit Discussion Openers

- How did you feel in your role? Why?
- If your group were to do this play again, what role would you choose? Why?
- What was your favorite part of the story? Why?
- What was your least favorite part of the story? Why?
- How does this play compare with the story in the Bible?